IDEAS IN PSYCHOANALYSIS

D1460581

Depression

Jeremy Holmes

Series editor: Ivan Ward

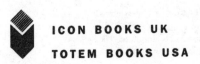

ICON BOOKS UK

TOTEM BOOKS USA

Published in the UK in 2002
by Icon Books Ltd., Grange Road,
Duxford, Cambridge CB2 4QF
E-mail: info@iconbooks.co.uk
www.iconbooks.co.uk

Sold in the UK, Europe, South Africa
and Asia by Faber and Faber Ltd.,
3 Queen Square, London WC1N 3AU
or their agents

Distributed in the UK, Europe,
South Africa and Asia by
Macmillan Distribution Ltd.,
Houndmills, Basingstoke RG21 6XS

Published in Australia in 2002
by Allen & Unwin Pty. Ltd.,
PO Box 8500, 83 Alexander Street,
Crows Nest, NSW 2065

Published in the USA in 2002
by Totem Books
Inquiries to: Icon Books Ltd.,
Grange Road, Duxford
Cambridge CB2 4QF, UK

Distributed to the trade in the USA
by National Book Network Inc.,
4720 Boston Way, Lanham,
Maryland 20706

Distributed in Canada by
Penguin Books Canada,
10 Alcorn Avenue, Suite 300,
Toronto, Ontario M4V 3B2

ISBN 1 84046 379 1

Typesetting by Hands Fotoset

Printed and bound in the UK by
Cox & Wyman Ltd., Reading

Introduction

Most of the time most of us feel mostly OK. We can sleep in our beds at night; our appetites – gustatory, sexual, exploratory – function normally; we can concentrate on whatever we happen to be doing, make plans, cope with setbacks and expect that things will turn out all right. We enjoy our family and friends and feel reasonably content with ourselves, accepting our shortcomings, aware of our strengths, able to forgive ourselves for our misdeeds and to celebrate our abilities and achievements – if we even bother to think about such things at all.

And yet, almost overnight, all this can go awry. For the depressed person, none of these simple securities can be taken for granted. Sleep becomes elusive, the future looks black or impossible, there is no pleasure in life, and to focus on a simple thing like reading a paper or watching a TV programme becomes problematic. Agitation or lethargy take over. As depression bites, our view of ourselves changes from acceptance and OK-ness to self-loathing, guilt at imagined sins of omission or commission and, ultimately, a wish to die.

Unlike most of the topics in this series, there is nothing specifically psychoanalytic about the notion of depression. Indeed, it can be argued that depression as we conceive of it today is as much a product of a subtle shaping of the way we view our emotional life by the pharmaceutical industry as it is of psychological medicine. The manufacturers of anti-depressants ensure that we conceptualise our distress as depression and thus have need of their products.

Freud, his contemporaries and predecessors wrote not about depression but 'melancholia' (literally 'black emotion'). They wanted to understand what today we would call psychotic depression. This condition, as contemporarily viewed, would be classified as Major Depressive Disorder or Manic Depressive Psychosis. These can truly be described as mental illnesses, distinct from the more common 'clinical depression' that is familiar to most of us today, whether as sufferers (one in four will be subject to depression at some point in our lives) or as professionals called upon to 'treat' this ubiquitous condition.

As a former neurologist, Freud's first foray into psychiatry was via 'hysteria' – i.e. dramatic physical symptoms thought to be psychological rather than 'organic' in origin – a condition that many psychiatric commentators consider almost to have vanished from the Western world. What we have instead in the West are depression and anxiety. It is worth noting, however, that in many cultures the predominant language through which emotional distress is expressed remains that of the body. The Yoruba of Nigeria, for example, have no word for depression, and patients whom a Western-trained doctor would consider as depressed present themselves in many parts of the developing world with such symptoms as 'heavy heart', abdominal pain and nausea, or general body weakness. Ethnographically, the notion of 'depression' as a purely psychological phenomenon is atypical.

Despite this caveat, depression will, according to the World Health Organisation, be the biggest cause of ill-health worldwide of any condition, physical or mental, by the year 2020. This represents a huge public health challenge. The aim of this essay is to describe current psychological approaches to depression, focusing mainly, but not exclusively, on psychoanalytic perspectives.

It starts by looking at the phenomenology of depression – patterns of depressive illness as described in literature and by sufferers – moves on to consider psychoanalytic and other theories of depression and in conclusion looks at psychological treatment methods in relation to depression, and the evidence for their effectiveness.

The Phenomenology of Depression

Churchill, a product of both paternal and maternal deprivation beyond the normal extent of even his era and class, dubbed his regularly recurring depression the 'black dog'. The writer William Styron's account of his depression is called, with Biblical and Miltonian echoes, *Darkness Visible*. He describes how:

... one bright day on a walk through the woods with my dog I heard a flock of Canada geese honking high above the trees ablaze with foliage; ordinarily a sight that would have exhilarated me, the flight of the birds caused me to stop, riveted with fear, and I stood stranded there, helpless, shivering, aware for the first time that I had been stricken by a serious illness ...[1]

Why do we associate depression, and indeed its close cousin death itself, with darkness? As children, we are alone in the dark, in peril of predation, unprotected; light is what nurtures and reassures us, literally through the sun's rays, and through the reflection of the mother's face and its smile, which lights up when she sees her infant. To be in the dark is to be unconnected, lost; light symbolises attachment and security, reaching out rather than closed-offness.

Styron describes the gulf (or 'glass wall', as many sufferers put it) that the depressive experiences between himself and all that is good and desirable. The light is there ('one *bright* day …'), but somehow it is out of reach, inaccessible. In Hamlet's passionate words:

I have of late (but wherefore I know not) lost all my mirth, forgone all custom of exercises; and indeed, it goes so heavily with my disposition that this goodly frame, the earth, seems to me a sterile promontory; this most excellent canopy, the air, look you – this brave o'erhanging firmament, this majestical roof fretted with golden fire

– why it appears no other thing to me than a foul and pestilent congregation of vapours.[2]

And:

How weary, stale, flat, and unprofitable
Seem to me all the uses of this world!
Fie on't! Oh fie! Tis an unweeded garden,
That grows to seed; things rank and gross in nature
Possess it merely...[3]

The depressive's anger and despair, his full knowledge of his condition, yet his inability to transcend it, his hatred of the beauty and majesty of the world, and his hatred of his hatred, is ineffably expressed here. As if in confirmation of the Freudian formulation of depression, Hamlet's despair is stimulated by his mother's evident sexuality – widowed, she rushes at once into the arms of her brother-in-law (in certain countries an accepted custom), leaving her son to wrestle with his jealousy and sense of exclusion and disgust. Depression, in this view, is no more or less than a narcissistic wound that reminds us of our frailty, impotence, inability to control those upon whom we depend and vulnerability to loss.

So depression is dark, lonely, disconnected. The depressed sufferer is hate-ful, in the double sense of being consumed with hate and also liable to be rejected. At a fundamental level, attachment – between the sufferer and his loved ones, or to life itself – is severed. Depressive anger and rage can be seen as an attempt to punish the world, and oneself, for having allowed this connection to break, as well as an envious attack on those who are not so afflicted. It is also a desperate attempt to re-establish connectedness. Obvious misery or an outburst of anger forces others to sit up and take notice; it is a plea and a warning – 'please don't reject me yet again'.

Keats' 'La Belle Dame sans Merci'[4] miraculously captures the bleak emptiness, and pervasive yearning for what is lost, of depression. The poet/protagonist questions a 'Knight-at-arms', found 'alone and palely loitering', on a 'bare hillside' where:

The sedge is wither'd from the lake
And no birds sing.

9

The 'Knight-at-arms' is lovesick. Like so many other 'pale kings and princes', he has fallen in love with the *Dame*, the merciless faery; she takes him to her 'elfin grot' and there 'he shut her wild wild eyes/With kisses four'. Once captured, she abandons him as she has her other unslaked suitors:

I saw their starv'd lips in the gloom
With horrid warning gaped wide,
And I awoke and found me here
On the cold hill's side.

To be depressed is to be starved, deprived of nurturance, to lose one's love object. Depression is the risk one takes in falling in love. For the infant, the mother who feeds and comforts is also the mother who can turn away and abandon her child. Seen in this way, depression is inherent in the human condition. This is expressed psychoanalytically in the notion of the oedipal situation, in which the growing child has to reconcile his or her desire for exclusive possession of the mother with the reality that he or she is a product of two parents' sexuality and

10

that she has to be shared with a father and her other children, present or to be conceived.

Clinical Profiles in Depression

Here are some fictitious but typical examples of the kinds of depression that present for help in psychiatric clinics.

Henry was a 40-year-old bank manager. A careful, meticulous man, he had worked his way up through the bank ranks until he headed up a large branch in a provincial town. As new methods of banking were introduced, he spent more and more time at the office in a desperate attempt to master the new procedures. He grew increasingly anxious, until one morning he awoke flooded with guilt and convinced that he was responsible for all his customers' bankruptcies, and that he would bring ruin upon his family.

Comment: This is a good example of 'psychotic depression', in which depressive guilt takes on delusional proportions. Obsessionality and a depressive tendency often go hand in hand.

Obsessional defences represent an attempt to impose order on an inherently chaotic world – to control the uncontrollable. The gap between a wished-for ideal state of harmonious relationships in a neat and orderly world, and the reality of tension and entropy is a constant source of conflict for the obsessive. Depressive guilt and self-blame, out of proportion to the responsibility that would be placed on the individual by society, often in a quasi-delusional way, maintain the fiction that all could be controlled if only one had found the right way to behave.

Amanda had a difficult childhood, being rejected by both parents and having been sexually abused by her grandfather between the ages of 10 and 16. Eventually, through her involvement in the church, she suddenly saw that his 'love' – however much she craved it as the only person who had ever shown an interest in her – was wrong. She then met her husband in her late teens, a headmaster, whom she revered and, as her own children were born, she gradually forgot her painful childhood, about which she had spoken to no one, not even her husband. But when she was in her 40s, her husband had a bad heart attack and was convalescent for several months. Soon after this, she became suicidal and spent several months in hospital, unable to cope and longing to die.

Comment: The origins of good self-esteem lie in a close and protective relationship with one's parents. Without such self-esteem, one is vulnerable to the difficulties and traumas that life throws up. In her depressive state, Amanda saw herself as a useless person, good only to be exploited by others. She had escaped from her difficult childhood through her relationship with her husband, but she remained subservient to and highly dependent on him. When he became ill, all her vulnerability and feelings of inadequacy returned. Her God had feet of clay; in her eyes, she was worthless and better off dead. She had lost her rock – all that remained was danger and inadequacy.

When Dave was 5, he and his brother were sent away to a children's home. He never really understood why – it was something to do with his Dad losing his job. His sisters remained behind in the family. Dave hated it in the home, and when revelations of sexual abuse of children in care appeared on TV, it brought back many painful memories of his own maltreatment. Dave was in the army at the time. He became deeply depressed and angry and started to hit his wife and two sons, and had to be discharged from his job. He hated himself for what he had done, and realised that in attacking his family he was undermining all that was good in his life.

Comment: Seen psychoanalytically, depressive self-hatred is a *displacement*. The rage Dave felt towards his parents for having abandoned him was directed not towards them, but at himself and his wife and sons. In his misery, he would talk to himself: 'You f...ing idiot. You useless sod. You don't deserve to be alive.' The apparently incomprehensible self-destructiveness of depression begins to make sense if it is assumed that it is directed not to the self, but to another by whom the sufferer feels let down.

Mary, aged 52, married with three children,

never really recovered after her mother's death. They had been close all her life – she was an only child of a single parent. She never knew her father. She would visit her mother most days and referred all important decisions to her. She had led a quiet life, never leaving her home town and marrying a boy she had been at school with. After her mother's death, she was unable to go to the funeral and could not go to her house or even drive down the street where it was. As the months went by, her grief gradually hardened into unremitting depression and her husband wondered if he would ever 'get his wife back'. Mary remained in a miserable, withdrawn, inert and frightened state in which she felt there was no meaning or purpose in life. She longed to 'join' her mum, and prayed every night as she went to bed that she would not wake up.

Comment: We see here a clear link between loss and depression. Mary is suffering from morbid grief. She cannot progress through the 'stages' of grief to a point of acceptance where she feels internally sustained by her lost 'object' – i.e. her mother. Her anxiety and habitual reliance on her mother as a base from which to deal with worry and mental pain mean that, in her bereaved state, she has no internal resources to help her get through the inevitable pain of loss. In her mind and in her behaviour, she avoids everything associated with the loss, and thus it remains 'un-metabolised', festering in her psyche, bringing her down, inaccessible for mental work. She is not necessarily angry with her mother for having 'left' her, but feels depleted and empty inside and cannot imagine regaining the confidence and strength that her mother's presence provided for her. Her only thought is to be reunited with the 'secure base' on which she depended so much. In fact, this degree of clinging and dependency would suggest that her attachment to her mother was not secure, but insecure in an ambivalent pattern. A securely attached person has, as an adult, an internal representation of those to whom they are close. Loss is bearable and surpassable because of this secure internal representation. In ambivalent attachment, this internal representation is problematic and the physical presence of the attachment figure is required in order to feel secure. When that person is lost, depression re-emerges.

Theories of Depression

Good psychological medicine adopts a comprehensive approach to understanding and treating mental distress. Due weight is given to biological, psychological and social factors and to their interactions. This 'biopsychosocial' perspective is the one adopted here and yields a multifaceted picture of the inner world of depression. The disorder of mood itself – feeling 'low', 'heavy', that 'everything is an effort', together with so-called *'biological'* features of weight loss, loss of libido, retardation, sleep disturbance and anhedonia (inability to experience pleasure) – lend themselves to a biological perspective that takes into account genetic predisposition, neurotransmitter disturbance and psychopharmacological treatments. *Psychological* approaches focus on guilt, suppressed anger, low self-esteem, hopelessness, inability to see a future and the vision through dark-tinted glasses that typifies the depressive world view.

Social theories of depression emphasise loss as

a crucial triggering factor for depression. This is either exacerbated by the absence of, or disturbance in, interpersonal relationships. This in turn feeds into lack of a sense of agency, and deficient social support and roles. Deprivation, prejudice and social exclusion provide a backdrop against which these immediate causes of depression all become far more likely.

Different approaches can also be classified according to whether they adopt an *intrapsychic* or *interpersonal* position – focusing either on the inner world of the sufferer or on her interactions with others. The former is that taken by biochemical, cognitive and, to some extent, psychoanalytic theories. The latter characterises some psychoanalytic approaches, as well as attachment-based and social perspectives.

Until recently, the worlds of biological psychiatry and psychoanalysis had little to say to each other, and what interchange there was seemed mostly negative. Neurobiology, with powerful links to the pharmaceutical industry, saw its province as the brain and focused almost exclusively on the biochemical changes in depression, without bothering too much about how such changes might come about, other than perhaps a vague nod in the direction of genetic propensity. This narrow 'medical model' saw depression as an illness, similar to diseases of the liver or the stomach. The counter-assertion that the idea of illness might be a socially constructed metaphor, if thought about at all, was dismissed as woolly-minded post-modernism. Psycho-analytic perspectives were equally hermetically sealed from advances in science, and tended to adopt equally simple (or simplistic) models concentrating exclusively on mental life, with little or no recognition of the role of the brain as a biological entity. Here the explanatory frame-work is almost exclusively on early childhood experience, and even the evident role of trauma in later life is problematic. These two positions can be caricatured as 'mindlessness' and 'brain-lessness'.

We are now entering a post-Cartesian era of 'neuropsychoanalysis'.[5] Recent studies suggest that mental experience can have structural impact on the brain, and it is more readily admitted by those who adopt a psychosocial position that the state of the brain will have powerful effects on mental experience. Intriguing links between physiological and psychological models of depression are beginning to emerge. It is likely that structural changes occur in the human infant's brain in response to early painful events, such as separations or losses. Prolonged stress, with concomitant high cortisol levels in the blood, produces changes in the hypothalamus, the part of the brain that controls the pituitary gland, an organ that affects much of the hormonal life of the individual.

One way in which neuropsychology has provided a collaborative impetus to psychological approaches to depression is in the elucidation of the traditional distinction between 'endogenous' and 'reactive' depression. The former, classical psychiatry asserts, is in some way 'intrinsic' to the individual, and can appear without any obvious external precipitant. By contrast, reactive depression, as its name implies, is a response to some form of environmental adversity – bereavement, loss of a job, divorce etc. The findings of social psychiatry research have blurred this distinction to some extent. It seems that 70 per cent of all depressions follow an adverse or loss event in the person's life, unrelated to the depression itself (some losses might be the consequence rather than the cause of depression if, for example, a depressed person lost his job because he was unable to function efficiently at work). Nevertheless, while most first episodes of depression do follow adverse life experience, subsequent ones often do not, appearing apparently 'out of the blue'. Also, there needs to be an explanation for why some individuals become depressed in response to loss, whereas others do not – clearly there are protective factors at work as well as vulnerability factors. Of these, the most significant may reside in the personality and its development – the province of psychoanalysis.

The psychoanalytic emphasis on the importance of early childhood experience is supported by the suggestion from neuroscience that early loss may *sensitise* receptor sites in the brain that can lead to vulnerability to depression later in life. There is a strong relationship between loss and the development of depression. The phenomenon of 'receptor kindling', derived from studies of epilepsy, is a useful paradigm to understand the mechanisms underlying this increased vulnerability. The more epileptic fits one has, the more likely one is to have more – previous fits sensitise the brain, so that eventually it takes no more than a small stimulus to 'kindle' the onset of a major fit. By analogy, repeated early trauma may 'set' the brain in such a state that, in later life, ideas or images that may appear only distantly connected to the theme of loss might be sufficient to tip the neurochemical system into a depressed state. This model goes some way to explain the psychoanalytic observation that an imagined or a symbolic loss is as potent a stressor in provoking depression as a real loss.

Psychoanalytic Models of Depression

Freud's early follower, Karl Abraham, first set Freud thinking about the origins of melancholia.[6] Abraham drew Freud's attention to the obvious parallels between the state of grief and the feelings and behaviours that characterise depression. He focused on two main problems in trying to understand the inner world of depression. First, if grief and depression are similar, and grief is a response to loss, what exactly is it that has been lost in depression? Second, why should an individual turn against himself in this way? He was thinking here of the puzzling delusional self-reproaches seen in melancholic depression. The bank manager, for instance, in the first example above, genuinely believed that his presumed misdemeanours were responsible for the downturn in the world economy that happened around the time of his illness.

Freud's answer to both these points is as follows:

... the self-reproaches with which these sufferers torment themselves so mercilessly actually relate to another person, to the sexual object they have lost or whom they have ceased to value on account of some fault ... the melancholic has ... by a process which we must call 'narcissistic identification' set up the object within the ego itself, projected it onto the ego ... the ego is then treated as though it were the abandoned object; it suffers all the revengeful and aggressive

treatment which is designed for the object ... In melancholia ... a feature of the emotional life ... we are accustomed to call ambivalence comes markedly to the fore; by this we mean directing antithetical feelings (affectionate and hostile) towards the same person.[7]

The origins of depression in this model start with an ambivalent relationship to a lost object. This could date back to an unresolved oedipal dilemma, in which the toddler both loves and hates the mother, whom he feels has abandoned him in favour of a subsequent child or her sexual partner. (This situation applies equally to either sex.) This ambivalence interferes with the normal mourning process by which a lost object is idealised and incorporated into the self (or the ego, as Freud called it). The potential depressive then has within himself, and as part of himself, an object about which he has mixed feelings: 'the shadow of the object has fallen upon the ego'.[8] He has made a narcissistic identification with an ambivalently held object. His self-esteem is compromised because part of his self contains elements that he hates. He is therefore vulnerable to depression, especially if a loss or slight in adult life throws him back in a regressive way to the primal loss with which he has been unable to come to terms. The 'orality' of the depressive, the refusal to eat or voracious bingeing ('comfort eating') are manifestations of this regression, in which the nursing infant, as it were, in his mind 'destroys' the very breast that he loves and on which he depends.

Freud's famous 'Mourning and Melancholia' paper[8] was seminal, not just because of its ingenious explanation for the self-reproaches of the melancholic, but because it heralded the beginnings of an 'object relations' metapsychology. In contrast to Freud's earlier theories, the internal world no longer consists of drives and defences, but is *populated* by internal representations of the individual and his relationships – self in relation to mother and father, father in relation to self and so on. It was but a small step from here for Freud to move from his early 'topographical model' of conscious, preconscious and unconscious to the 'structural model' of ego, id and superego.[9] The superego, in particular, came to be seen as the repository of internalised ideals and values acquired from relationships with parents and other authority figures upon whom the individual depends.

Melanie Klein, like Freud, was influenced by Abraham's ideas. She took up the baton of object relations and brought her own ideas to the understanding of depression. In her model, however, ambivalence and its transcendence came to reflect a central theme of the human condition. Like Abraham, and indeed all the early analysts, she sought 'fixation points' in child development that would parallel and underlie adult psychological difficulties.

Through her observations of infants and small children, she claimed that children were frequently subject to periods of sadness:

... the change between excessive high spirits and extreme wretchedness, which is a characteristic of melancholic disorders [i.e. manic-depression], *is regularly found in children.*[10]

With typical brilliance (but equally typical disregard for any sort of systematic evidence), she then theorised that there is a development from the 'paranoid-schizoid position' in the early months of life to the 'depressive position' somewhere between the middle and the end of the first year of life. Reaching the depressive position is a positive developmental step, in that it represents the moment at which the child realises that the frustrating absent mother is one and the same as the nurturing loving caregiver. This depressive feeling also leads to an acknowledgement of guilt that one has hated the person one also loves. It also is accompanied by a particular type of anxiety – the fear that one's aggression will destroy or drive away the object.

The Kleinian developmental model suggests two types of depression. The first is a paranoid-tinged feeling based on splitting, in which one is trapped in a world of loss, envy and despair, irretrievably separated from the good things of life. There is no sense of a holding environment[11] within which the depressive feelings can be mitigated or transcended.

The second is a sense of sadness or 'grounded grief', representing a move towards maturity, and is often seen in patients undergoing dynamic psychotherapy as they begin to diminish acting

out behaviour and to contain their more difficult emotions. The latter view justifies the psychoanalytic aphorism 'where there's depression
there's hope'. Klein developed the important
idea of 'reinstatement of the lost object' within
the psyche, so that if development is healthy,
or therapy successful, the individual feels the
object is secure inside the inner world, even
though lost in the outer world. Here love out-
weighs hate, and the pain and rage of grief can
have a healing or cleansing, rather than purely
destructive, aspect.

Freud and Klein emphasised the *narcissistic*
aspect to depression, in which the sufferer
becomes increasingly self-preoccupied and withdrawn from relationship with others. The idea
of a 'narcissistic wound' lying at the heart of
depression explains some of the phenomena
already described, e.g. taking every slight or loss
'personally' (much emphasised by cognitive
behavioural approaches to depression, see below).

The link between narcissism and the oedipal
situation emerges in Freud's idea that 'fear of
success' can be a significant precipitant of depression – as indeed it was when he himself had the

chance to go to Athens, and promptly fell into a depression. He attributed this to his fear of 'going further than the father' – i.e. the little boy longs to supersede his father in the eyes of his mother, but if he were to do so in reality he would immediately be stricken with anxiety. When worldly achievement is striven for as an antidote to feelings of inadequacy, accomplishment may evoke not joy but a sense of hollowness and ashes. This may, in part, be due to Freud's idea of success as inevitably involving competition and therefore the vanquishing of an adversary on whom, unconsciously, one may depend – i.e. the father. At the same time, external acclaim for the depressive has at best only a short-lived impact on inner feelings of emptiness and unlovableness. There may be an unremitting cycle in which yet another achievement 'fix' is needed in order to counteract the inevitable low that follows each success.

The neo-Kleinian Robert Caper[12] contrasts the narcissistic depression of the paranoid-schizoid state with that of the depressive position. In paranoid-schizoid states, the ego is fused with that of the object, and cannot recognize or accept the fact that the object is separate from itself. Depression centres around the fear of being taken over by the object, with concomitant feelings of depletion and emptiness of the self. In depressive-position thinking, by contrast, the object is separate and this allows for healthy mourning.

Sam arrived at his psychotherapy session in a state of extreme agitation. He was in his smart clothes and had just been to a funeral of a close friend. He had suffered from depression for most of his life, his mother having died when he was 2 and, after a brief period with his grandmother, having been brought up by a cruel, abusive and collusive father and stepmother. Despite his depressive tendencies, he had managed to work successfully as a solicitor and, by being in a state of emotional withdrawal, to hide his misery from the world, including his rather distant wife, herself a successful career woman. At the funeral, the widow of the deceased had read out a poem about the primroses that she and her husband had enjoyed as they returned each year, and expressing her sorrow that he was a primrose whose bloom would not appear on the following year. Sam revealed that rather than being touched and tearful in response to this image, as were the other mourners, he had felt 'turned to stone': utterly empty, bleak and cut off from everyone. In addition, he said that he felt that the therapy was going nowhere, and that was entirely his fault.

Comment: For those in a state of depressive-position grief, the image of the poem was moving and comforting. Their objects were experienced as separate, and they could allow them to come and go – or so Sam imagined. Loss is painful and sad – next year there will be one less primrose – but the self will remain intact despite the loss. The image of the loved one is represented in the poem, and the memory of the dead man lives on in the internal world. Any resentment or hatred towards him is far out-weighed by love – as expressed in the Latin tag 'de mortuis nihil nisi bonum'.[13] For Sam it was quite otherwise. Operating at a primitive paranoid-schizoid level of mental functioning, he was thrown back to his 2-year-old self, forcibly torn from a mother from whom he had not at that developmental stage separated himself. She was part of him and he was part of her. For him, loss meant to be 'ripped asunder'. He could not separate himself sufficiently from his object to be able to see that the primal loss and any subsequent losses were unconnected with any feelings that he might or might not have. Fused with his object, every loss and setback was inevitably his 'fault'.

Bob grew up in a household dominated by loss: his father had died in the war when he was 2, his mother never remarried and remained in a state of reverential grief until her own death when Bob was 15. He was then looked after by his older sister, until a minor misdemeanour took him into an approved school, where he was sexually maltreated by the staff and bullied by his peers. On release, he got a steady job and worked his way up through the ranks of the firm, eventually to become works manager. He married and soon divorced, but remained feeling guilty and unable to let his first wife go in his mind. Eventually, he remarried a highly subservient woman older than himself, whom he controlled and kept in the dark about much of his inner and even outer life. His depression began when the firm went into receivership. An obsessional man, a workaholic, with immense feel for detail but difficulty in making strategic decisions, he blamed himself entirely for the firm's failure. The course of his therapy centred around the idea of the object as having a life of its own, helping him to see that the firm's demise might well have happened whatever his efforts. A similar consideration applied to allowing his wife to visit her relatives when she wanted and to express her own opinions. The therapist felt similarly controlled and compromised by him; breakthroughs occurred when he and Bob could 'agree to differ' and come to the conclusion that they could 'both be right' about some disputed point.

Comment: Bob illustrates many features of paranoid-schizoid depression: his dead father was never forgiven for having died; the object is not separate from the self and so cannot be separated from it; life cannot go on freely but is always anchored in the past and un-mourned ties. The collapse of his firm produced similar reactions to the death of his father and the ending of his marriage: he *was* his factory and if it went under then so too must he. As therapy progressed, he moved more towards a depressive-position type of melancholy, in which he could see that his simultaneous love and hate of the same object was what made life so difficult. He loved his wife and wanted her to feel free to come and go as she pleased, but was terrified that if he were to relinquish his control over her, he would lose his attachment to her. He remained depressed, albeit less intensely so, since he felt he was staying alive for her sake, and that if he could have his own way his life would be worthless. Thus, he could not fully love his object, but rather felt bound to it by ties of duty, which set up a hatred that was not fully outweighed by love. All this was at an unconscious and inferential level and, if asked, he would with entire honesty have said that he had no hatred for his wife at all – as indeed he did not in his conscious mind.

Moving from an intrapsychic to a more relational focus, Jonathan Pedder[14] has linked

Kleinian ideas about depression with the findings of social psychiatry research. George Brown and Tirril Harris[15] found that early loss of the mother is a significant vulnerability factor for depression in later life. For them, self-esteem is the crucial issue in depression – those that can maintain good self-esteem in the face of loss are protected from depression, even though they may experience intense sadness and grief. Self-esteem, according to Pedder, implies an internal object relationship in which one part of the self is 'held' lovingly by another. This in turn depends on having been 'held' (both literally and metaphorically) lovingly by a caregiver in the past. If, through death or separation, or illness (e.g. maternal depression), that process has been compromised, then the individual's capacity to hold himself in good regard will be in jeopardy. He will not be able to celebrate what is good about himself, or to mourn his failings and accept his weaknesses. He will always be striving for a perfection – an idealised relationship – which can never be achieved.

Another important psychoanalytic idea about depression concerns the role of the superego.

Many depressed patients report a lack of unconditional love from their parents, or a feeling of never being quite good enough, however hard they try. A typical story is the child who came home from school having got 99 per cent in a maths test – only to be told by her father (here it is usually the father who is at fault) that he expected nothing less than 100 per cent! This process may be internalised in the form of a *harsh superego* constantly criticising the sufferer and reinforcing a sense of failure. While this may indeed represent the real strictures of controlling and perfectionistic parents, it may also emanate from the depressed person himself, as feelings of disappointment and anger are projected into parental figures.

This notion of *disappointment* was further developed by Edith Jacobson[16] in an attempt to account for the pervasive low self-esteem of the depressive. Not all mental pain is associated with such gross traumata as loss of a parent or sexual abuse. Neglect – a much-overlooked form of poor parenting – can lead to chronic feelings of being let down and disappointed. Jacobson, picking up on Freud's view of depression as a 'narcissistic disorder' (i.e. one that reawakens states of mind in which the individual is, like an infant in early childhood, still wrapped up in himself), argues that if loss or disappointment occur in early childhood, before self and object representations have been fully differentiated, this creates a heightened vulnerability to loss in later life. In this situation, when the object *is* lost, it feels as though part of the self has been destroyed as well.

Relational/Social/Attachment Models

Social psychiatry takes it as axiomatic that humans are social animals and that self-esteem depends on feeling part of a network whose members play reciprocally reinforcing roles. Biological, and to some extent cognitive, models of depression concentrate on the individual and his or her internal workings, be they biochemical or intrapsychic. Social models are essentially interpersonal. They start from the position that such a patterned behavioural response as depression, however apparently disadvantageous to the individual, must have adaptive significance and be comprehensible from an evolutionary perspective.

The 'social ranking' theory of depression sees depressive symptomatology in terms of dominance hierarchies within human groups[17] that exist, albeit often in latent or unacknowledged ways, in all human societies, at both a local level (e.g. the 'pecking order' in an office) and nationally (differences in power, wealth, influence etc.). When individuals lose status, e.g. through separation from a partner or loss of 'resource holding potential' (loss of a job, loss of money or a home, loss of sexual attractiveness through ageing, disfigurement etc.), they are vulnerable to aggression and displacement or expulsion from high-ranking types within the group. Social ranking theory argues that the depressive response provides a period of withdrawal in which an individual whose status has declined through loss can slide quietly down the dominance ladder without provoking attack and, with reduced activity and appetite, consume only modest resources in a way that would not provoke hostility from competitors. This enforced hibernation is thus protective and enables sufferers to husband their resources until they are once more ready to enter the fray.

The social ranking hypothesis fits well with the psychoanalytic model. Freud was a Darwinian, and would probably have been attracted to the notion that such a common phenomenon as depression was a product of our evolutionary inheritance. On the other hand, Freud took from Darwin the idea of the struggle for survival and transposed it to the inner world. For him, depression is a manifestation of the conflict between aggression and dependency – a fear of biting the hand that feeds. Even the notion of 'fear of success' can be seen as arising from awareness of the envy that advance inevitably arouses in those less successful. Modern evolutionary psychology, however, emphasises a more adaptational aspect to depression. Contemporary theory focuses less on the survival of the fittest and more on a necessary withdrawal while new resources are husbanded – a *reculer pour mieux sauter*. Each leads to differing therapeutic strategies. For classical psychoanalysis, conflict and aggression need to come out into the open; reassurance and support are anathema. Contemporary social ranking theory endorses support as part of the temporary moratorium that depression demands when status is lost.

Attachment theory combines psychoanalytic and social perspectives. John Bowlby's attachment theory[18,19] puts loss as the central theme in his theorising about depression. For Bowlby, good self-esteem and healthy curiosity depend on secure attachment. Attachment provides the necessary secure base that underlies healthy mental functioning and is ideally directed to a trusted other – usually a parent or spouse – but may also be extended to a particular role, job, social group or skill. If the secure base is lost, for example through death of a spouse or divorce, or through unemployment, then the affected individual will undergo a grief/mourning response. Bowlby sees grief in terms of irretrievable separation. Many of the phenomena of grief can be understood as desperate attempts to become reunited with a secure base. Since connectedness and attachment are intrinsic to our biological nature, attachment theory, like Kleinian theory, sees depression as an inevitable consequence of human relatedness. Those who cannot feel physical pain, for example people suffering from leprosy, might at first sight appear to be blessed – who would want to suffer pain if it could be avoided? In fact, they are grossly disadvantaged and frequently end up with severely damaged extremities. Similarly, the mental pain of depression is a concomitant of relatedness. Those who cannot feel mental pain are also deprived of the security and pleasures of intimacy.

In the 'environment of evolutionary adaptation', which for humans was the African savannah, an infant separated from its caregiver was at great risk of predation. Anxiety, crying, searching and anger all work to promote reunion with the secure base, and other activities such as feeding are shelved until security is re-established. When one is bereaved, the first response is denial – an attempt within one's mind to hold onto the status quo ante, in which the secure base relationship is still intact. This may be adaptive in situations of extreme danger, where the affected individuals have to remove themselves from peril before they can begin to deal with the situation they are in – such as soldiers wounded in battle who feel no pain until they reach the field ambulance station.

Even if the bare facts of loss are accepted intellectually, the bereaved individual continues to 'rewrite history' in his mind as he goes over and over the events leading up to the loss, trying to create scenarios with a different ending, always trying to re-find his lost loved one. During this phase, the sufferer may be in a state of emotional blunting. Self-blame can be seen as an omnipotent attempt to gain control over what is, in reality, an irretrievable and probably random act of fate: 'if only I had acted differently – visited my dying mother the day before, worked harder at my job so that bankruptcy could have been avoided – then this would never have happened'. This can be seen as a version of the narcissism that Freud was so struck by. Feelings of collapse and loss of control, and overwhelming sadness and weeping are common here, as the sufferer begins to 'bargain' with fate or God: 'I promise to be good, if only you will bring back my lover.'

Graham Greene, in *The End of the Affair*,[20] explores this theme from a Catholic perspective.

The protagonist, a Greene-like writer, starts a wartime affair with the wife of a stuffed shirt and rather impotent acquaintance. During an air raid, there is a direct hit on the house where they are sleeping together. During the ensuing chaos, the adulterous wife thinks her husband is dead. A lapsed Catholic, she then makes a classic grief bargain with God. If only her lover can be miraculously restored to life, she will give up a relationship that she knows is wrong and hurtful to her husband. The irony is that she still cannot avoid loss: she has to give up her relationship in return for his being alive, and it later turns out that she is suffering from terminal cancer.

A separated child in hospital was found by Bowlby to enter a state of despair – emotional withdrawal and listlessness – when the fact that the loss cannot be retrieved sinks in. Similarly, the bereaved person goes through a phase of despair before, little by little, the possibility of repair and new life begins to arise in his mind. Only then can new attachments be formed, the lost loved one reinstated safely within the inner world.

The social model takes this mourning process

as a paradigm for the phenomena of depression. The sufferer has to be helped to grieve his losses in the benign presence of a therapist, who provides a temporary secure base that helps the depressed subject face up to his feelings of anger and despair and terror.

Indeed, mourning may shade off into depression and, if it is delayed or prolonged, a clinical picture indistinguishable from depression may develop. Equally, as already suggested, depression may be the presenting manifestation of a mourning that has been suppressed or with which the sufferer has been unable to come to terms. Attachment Theory can be helpful in trying to pinpoint the circumstances in which this is more or less likely to occur. Where the relationship between the sufferer and his lost loved one has been 'insecure' (in attachment terms) rather than secure, impaired grief is most likely. There are two main patterns of insecure attachment. In 'insecure-avoidant' individuals, emotional reactivity is 'hypo-activated' (i.e. tuned down); when bereaved, they may enter a state of chronic emotional blunting. The converse is 'insecure-ambivalent' or a 'hyperactivated' state, in which the mourning individual remains inconsolable. Here they feel chronically overwhelmed with sadness and unable to move on.

The notion of insecure attachment can illuminate situations in which depression arises in troubled relationships rather than when there is actual bereavement through death or separation. For example, one member of a couple may 'carry' the depression for both of them, through the phenomenon of 'projective identification' in which unwanted psychic experience is unconsciously transmitted from one individual to another. Both may feel empty and low in self-esteem in a scenario in which the couple seem unable to separate for fear of feelings of emptiness and loneliness, or to get close for fear of being overwhelmed by one another's negative emotions. In another common interpersonal scenario, there is a vicious circle in which one member of the couple becomes mildly depressed, at which point the spouse takes over his or her role within the family, which then reinforces the sufferer's sense of uselessness and irrelevance, leading to a further fall in social ranking, more depressive feelings, and so on.

In such couples there is often an element of the *sadomasochism* or dominance-submission which can typify depressive relationships, in which depressed patients appear to seek out a victim role, and to be punishing those around them with their misery and hopelessness. From an attachment perspective, failure of a more reciprocal secure type of attachment can lead to a switch into an insecure bullied/clinging pattern in order to maintain some kind of connection to a secure base, however compromised.

Cognitive-Behavioural Models

Cognitive behavioural therapy is often postulated as antithetical to psychoanalytic approaches, but its founder, Aaron Beck, was trained as a psychoanalyst, and there is increasing interest in integrative approaches to psychotherapy[21] and developing dialogue between previously rival models. In practice, it is likely that many psychoanalytic therapists, consciously or unwittingly, at times use cognitive interventions with their clients, and conversely that cognitive therapists are increasingly taking account of psycho-analytic themes such as transference.

Many sufferers blame their depression on adverse circumstances, and social psychiatric research suggests that they are right to do so, since those suffering from depression are five times more likely to have experienced an adverse loss-like event in the previous year than those who do not become depressed. Nevertheless, the majority of those who experience such losses do not become depressed, which implies that factors other than circumstance also play their part. 'Resilience' seems to be linked to personality factors, in part genetic, in part the product of favourable developmental experiences. Thus recent research suggests that some individuals may be more prone to adverse life events than others, and that this tendency has, in part at least, a genetic basis, presumably related to the propensity for risk-taking, which although it yields many benefits also exposes the individual to more potential for hazard and loss.

Cognitive therapy for depression[22] takes as its starting point the perspective implied in Epictetus's famous statement that men are troubled not so much by things, as their perception of things. What we make of what we are made of is what determines whether or not we become depressed in the face of adversity.

Cognitive therapy identifies a particular set of negativistic ideas and attitudes that are characteristic of depression. They are 'cognitive' in that they are held to be the product of faulty reasoning. The origin of this faulty logic is not an immediate focus in cognitive approaches (cognitive therapists adopt the position, to paraphrase Marx, that psychoanalysts have interpreted the world, but the point remains to change it). Here lies a possible rapprochement with psychoanalytic thinking. It is plausible that particular patterns of dysfunctional thinking and reasoning are deeply embedded in the mind and may have arisen as a result of repeated maladaptive childhood experience. Conversely – and here lies the main therapeutic thrust of cognitive behavioural therapies – repeated adaptive, positive actions or thoughts have the potential to change faulty cognitions. To return to Hamlet:

For use can almost change the stamp of nature

And master even the Devil or throw him out
With wondrous potency[23]

In Beck's model, depressed mood is the result of negative thinking rather than vice versa, and if faulty actions and their underlying logic can be corrected therapeutically, then mood will lift.

There are a number of typical patterns of negative thinking that present themselves as 'automatic thoughts', which intrude themselves on depressive sufferers and determine their outlook. Here too lies a link with psycho-analysis, since 'automatic thoughts' are often unconscious, or at least pre-conscious, and much of the work of cognitive therapy, as with psychoanalytic psychotherapy, consists in help-ing the sufferer to become more aware of these below-the-surface thoughts and assumptions.

Faulty reasoning in cognitive therapy is classi-fied under a number of headings:

- Arbitrary inference. This means interpreting an event in a negative way without consider-ing alternative explanations, e.g. 'the fact that my boyfriend didn't ring me last night *proves* that he doesn't care about me'. The patient will be asked to think of alternative explanations – he was out, the telephone didn't work, he was tired etc. Here low self-esteem both creates negative inferences but, in a vicious circle, also results from them. Psychoanalytically, this might be seen as regressing to primitive egocentric modes of thinking.

- Selective abstraction. Taking facts out of context – e.g. 'my wife goes out with her girlfriends every Wednesday night so she obviously doesn't want to spend time with me' – even though she may spend every other evening with her husband. Again this represents a narcissistic world view and one dominated by paranoid-schizoid thinking in which bad thoughts cannot be reconciled with soothing and positive possibilities.

- Over-generalisation. Taking one negative experience to represent the whole, e.g. 'when I asked for a date, she refused me, so I must be totally unattractive'. Here there are interesting links with the work of the psychoanalyst Ignacio Matte-Blanco.[24] He argued that the unconscious tends always to obscure differences, in a process that he called 'symmetric-isation', whereas the logical, conscious mind focuses on the asymmetry or differences between things. Healthy mental functioning involves striking a balance between the two, and the depressed person may be in the sway of symmetricisation.

- Personalisation. Adverse experiences are interpreted self-referentially, e.g. 'the fact that my son is doing badly at school must be due to me being a bad parent'. This kind of thinking clearly underlies many of the guilty feelings that dog the depressive. Again they imply a self-centred mind-set that characterises the paranoid-schizoid position.

- Minimisation and maximisation. Negative events are blown up out of proportion while successes are diminished in importance.

- Dichotomous thinking. Things are seen in black-or-white terms – e.g. 'If I make a mistake, that proves I am a total failure.' This relates to the perfectionistic aspect of depression mentioned earlier, in which feelings of impotence and marginalisation are dealt with by an obsessional need to be in total control, and again represents a failure to asymmetricise.

Cognitive approaches see mental structures in terms of a hierarchy, summarised in the acronym 'EARS' – Expectations, Assumptions, Rules and Schemata. These move from relatively superficial and consciousness-accessible expectations and assumptions, to deeply ingrained and less accessible schemata. As suggested already, the latter are not too far removed from the psychoanalytic notion of internal objects and their relationships or unconscious phantasies. Schemata comprise a set of 'meta-rules' that determine one's fundamental outlook on life, and that in the depressed person might take the form of self-statements such as 'what ever you do you are bound to fail', 'you are a waste of space', 'you will never make another person happy', etc. Although these deep assumptions may be based in adverse experience, from a psychoanalytic perspective they will be coloured by unconscious phantasy, and so 'unrealistic' in the sense of exaggerated or excessively 'symmetrical' (in Matte-Blanco's terms, see above).

John Teasdale and his co-workers[24] argue that, in chronic and severe depression, therapy has to reach and challenge these deeper levels if it is to be successful, and here too the links with psychoanalytic thinking are clear.

Another influential cognitive theory of depression flows from the work of Martin Seligman,[26] who famously coined the phrase 'learned helplessness' to describe experimental situations in which animals, in this case dogs, unable to fathom or control a reward–punishment schedule, 'gave up' in a way that was reminiscent of the behaviour of depressed patients. A key assumption here is that self-esteem depends on a sense of mastery and the capacity to influence ones' environment. Put psychoanalytically, the depressed oedipal child feels impotent and psychologically castrated. He may develop various forms of omnipotent thinking in compensation; if things go well, as development proceeds he begins to acquire real potency and a sense of his resource-holding potential. If there are setbacks, or his positive attributes are not fostered, then he will be liable to depression when faced with loss, and resort first to omnipotent thinking and then to the

given up/give up position of learned helplessness. As with the vicious circle of arbitrary inference, the withdrawal and inertia of depression
itself reinforces the helplessness/hopelessness
that may have initiated the illness in the first place.

Suicide and Depression

The theme of suicide is never far away in
working with depressed patients. The therapist
will need to be at home with discussion of
suicide and its possible consequences. A full
discussion of the psychotherapy of suicide is
beyond the scope of this essay, but a few
remarks are in order. Karl Menninger (1933)
believed that three wishes might contribute
towards a suicidal act – the wish to *kill*, the wish
to *be killed* and the wish to *die*. The wish to kill
may not only be directed towards an internal
object but, as in the case of the suicide bomber, is
often designed to destroy the lives of the sur-
vivors in one final act of revenge, a catastrophic
settling of scores. It is sometimes helpful to
remind suicidal patients that if they kill themselves, their mental pain will not disappear
altogether, but outlive them, transferred to their

loved ones who will continue to suffer until their death.

The wish to be killed and the wish to die are clearly related. In both cases, there is an implied passivity, and many depressed patients say something along the lines of 'I haven't got the guts to kill myself, but if I were to go to sleep and not wake up in the morning it would be a wonderful release.' The wish to be killed addresses the guilt and need for punishment that goes with depression – a feeling that one doesn't deserve to live, and possibly an implied punishment for loved ones who, in the mind of the suicidal depressive 'would be better off without me'. The wish to die ultimately is an expression of the intense mental pain associated with depression. One sufferer who had also had a coronary thrombosis (coronary artery disease appears to be more common in those with depressive and aggressive tendencies) claimed that the mental pain of depression far outweighed the physical pain of a coronary. The depressed person feels utterly trapped with his misery. The thought of death can be the only escape route from this choiceless suffering.

Suicide can be viewed as a form of 'acting out' – i.e. the behavioural and concrete ful-filment of an inner phantasy. Robert Hale[27] introduces the idea of a suicide phantasy, which involves an ambivalent relationship between the part of the self that will survive, the 'surviving self', and the body, which is identified with an object that has to die. An important part of the phantasy is that of the pleasurable survival of an essential part of the self. The unbearable loss of a loved one and the phantasy of reunion can in themselves lead to suicide, especially where there has been a highly dependent relationship. Suicide can, in a perverse way, appear as a 'solution' to the problem of irretrievable separ-ation mentioned earlier. Many suicidal patients reveal strong and unresolved dependency needs towards a lost object; suicide may be viewed as a regressive wish for reunion with a lost maternal figure. One reading of Keats' 'La Belle Dame sans Merci' would be to see it as a death-dream of a rejected suitor, who would rather remain in the suspended animation of post-suicidal 'living' than accept that his love was gone for ever. As Glen Gabbard comments, 'When an individual's

self-esteem and self-integrity depend on attachment to a lost object, suicide may seem to be the
only way to restore self-cohesion.'[28]

Finally, it is important never to assume that
the suicidal person wants *only* to die, nor to
think that someone who makes superficial cuts
on her wrists is not suicidal and simply 'drawing
attention to herself', or making a bid for help. It
is better to work on the assumption that such
people *both* want to die *and* want to live, but
that the balance between these poles varies from
time to time and from person to person. In other
words, ambivalence is universal, and there is
always a mixture of love and hate. It is the job
of the therapist to try to help the patient see
the object of his love and hate as separate from
himself, and to try to tip the balance in favour
of love and concern, rather than the wish to
destroy the object.

Postnatal Depression

Another important topic that can only be briefly
mentioned is that of postnatal depression.
Physiological factors play an important part in
triggering this common and distressing condition

– it is more common in women who have had prolonged or complicated labours. In Donald Winnicott's notion of 'primary maternal pre-occupation',[29] all thought and activity becomes centred on the baby. The mother's own experience of mothering is, through 'implicit memory' or 'memory in the body', reawakened. If those memories are problematic, say through grandmaternal depression or separation, then this may impact on the next generation. In puerperal depression, the mother may experience herself as inadequate, lacking in 'maternal feelings', hostile to the baby or afraid that she will harm it. The role of the father and/or grandmother in providing a safe containing network around the feeding mother is also important and depression around childbirth is more common in the absence of such support. These feelings may assume psychotic proportions in some cases.

The mere fact of parenthood is an expression of narcissism and yet demands a transcendence of it. Proud mothers have to put their own needs to one side in order to attend to their babies. One new mother who suffered from obsessive-compulsive disorder became depressed and guilty as she struggled with her resentment at the baby who introduced, as she saw it, such chaos into her neatly ordered world. His cries were his way of insisting that his needs took precedence over hers; she felt that she had to attend to her own health needs if she was to survive at all. The price she paid for this 'selfishness' was guilt and depression.

Psychoanalytic Techniques in Depression

Psychoanalytic psychotherapy does not specify particular therapeutic techniques for depressed patients. However, certain principles will govern the evolution of the transference in working with depression. First, as in any therapy, there is the need to form a good working alliance. This will be confounded by three types of counter-transference emotion: despair, irritation and the desire to nurture the patient.

First, it is the therapist's job to hold on to hope in the early stages of therapy. In the Klein–Bion model, this requires the therapist, using depressive-position thinking to 'metabolise' and 'detoxify' feelings of hopelessness that are projected into her. Second, resentment and exasperation are often, but not invariably, features of working with depressed patients. Here it is tempting to bully patients into seeing how distorted their worldview is, and how they neglect or actively destroy the good things about themselves. This too must be resisted, as it recreates the sadomasochistic structure that characterises the patient's inner world, and substitutes dominance/submission for empathic responsiveness. Third, the pity and longing to help that some depressed patients evoke have to be tempered with attention to boundaries – it is all too easy to become sucked into the regressed inner world of the depressive, in which the capacity to think, and so to rise above pain, has been abandoned.

In oedipal terms, there must always be a third term or an external viewpoint from which the depressed feelings can more objectively be viewed. Winnicott's description of healthy 'hate in the counter-transference'[30] makes a powerful case for both maintaining one's integrity as a therapist at the same time as being able to identify with the patient's distress.

For the psychoanalytic psychotherapist working with depressed patients, a central theme will inevitably be that of loss, present and past. There will be the precipitating loss that has led to the current depression, but it is equally important to seek out prior episodes of loss or abandonment that may well have been suppressed and inadequately grieved. This may centre on a parent who has abandoned the patient, the arrival of a displacing sibling or the death of a loved grandparent. In each case, the therapist will try to relate the devastating response to the immediate situation to an earlier stage of the patients' lives, where their vulnerability was at its greatest and yet their capacity to control their environment was limited. The passivity, helplessness and the 'trapped' feeling of depression will be reframed in the light of this regression to an earlier loss.

While focusing in this way on the content of the patient's biography, the therapist will also try to provide a secure, responsive and reliable base from which he or she can begin to work through the grief associated with disappointment. Ultimately, the task of the therapy is to help the patient internalise a more benign version of the abandoning object – to see, for example, that parents whose care was so inadequate were themselves struggling with their own difficulties. Pedder identifies three situations where this is particularly difficult: when a parent disappears without trace during childhood, when a spouse abandons his or her partner and when a therapist has terminated working with a patient for no apparent reason.[31] In all three cases, it is extremely difficult to internalise a benign version of the abandoning object. The loss appears arbitrary, cruel and unpremeditated. The sufferer will often assume that it is something he or she has 'done'.

In recovery, a more balanced version of the intense guilt felt by depressed patients will also be found. Patients no longer blame themselves omnipotently for 'everything', while at the same time begin to take appropriate responsibility for the part they play in the maintenance of their depression, as suggested in the Kleinian idea of the depressive position. Thus, for example, an abandoned spouse may finally be able to look at ways in which he or she has driven the partner away and, in addition, while remaining appropriately angry, come to see that there were some happy times between them as well as miserable ones.

Psychodynamic-interpersonal therapy is another generic therapy that has been used extensively to treat mild to moderate depression.[32] Here, the emphasis is especially on empathic responses by the therapist, and on helping the patient to find metaphors to capture the essence of his feelings, however gloomy. Transferential feelings of rejection and loss in relation to the therapy itself (e.g. at the time of the therapist's holiday breaks) are fore-grounded in the hope that they can be worked through with appropriate sadness and anger, rather than reinforcing depressive affects. For example, it is typical of 'insecure-avoidant' patients, who dampen down their emotions in the interests of emotional security, that they will show or experience little or no reaction to the therapist's breaks: 'Why do you keep going on about my supposed anger about your holidays? Actually I don't feel anything about it. You are a professional and are entitled to leave as much as anyone.' Later, such a patient may begin to admit that he does miss his therapist while he is away and come to see how, for example, he embarked on a disastrous affair during the break with the aim of providing temporary comfort, while unconsciously punishing the therapist for his disloyalty by being self-destructive.

A key psychoanalytic theme in the recovery from depression is that of reparation. For the depressive, the inner world is shattered and the external world may appear so too – literally in the case of the depressed adolescent male who 'trashes' his room in a state of drunken or drug-induced despair. If therapy is successful, destruction and loss can be overcome by the painful, but at times joyous, process of repair and rebuilding. As D.H. Lawrence put in his poem 'Manifesto', celebrating the end of an appalling series of rows with his wife in the collection *Look! We Have Come Through*:

I want her to touch me at last, ah, on the root
    and quick of my darkness
And perish on me, as I have perished on her.
Then we shall be two and distinct, we shall have
    our separate being.[33]

This poem with its sexual overtones can be read as a celebration of the move from paranoid-schizoid to depressive thinking, from fusion to individuation – a synthesis of destruction into creativity, a pruning back that allows for the emergence of new growth.

The sensitive therapist is always on the look-out for signs of incipient reparation in patients. This may take the form of dreams of new growth, or of building sites, architectural construction, preparing delicious meals, or of burgeoning evidence of creativity in the arts or DIY – or even such simple decisions as to 'finally go to the dentist and get my teeth seen to'!

Group analytic techniques can be used effectively in the treatment of depression. Of well-known therapeutic factors in group analysis, the instillation of hope, universality, interpersonal learning and group cohesiveness will all in different ways help the depressive to overcome his sense of isolation and alienation from society.

Cognitive Techniques in Depression

Cognitive therapy was devised originally as a treatment for depressed patients, but has now widened greatly in scope. As cognitive-*behavioural* therapy (CBT), it also incorporates behavioural techniques that are as important in helping depressed patients as are the strictly cognitive components of the therapy. Some key components of CBT treatment for depression include:

- Keeping a mood diary, so the patient can begin to identify variations in mood through the day, and the triggers that lead to perpetuation of their misery. A mood diary also helps with *objectification* and distancing from the depressed mood itself, thus creating the beginnings of mastery.
- Identifying '*automatic thoughts*' as they arise in relation to difficult everyday situations. The patient, as a 'scientist collaborator', is then helped to question and challenge the basis for these thoughts and to practice substituting alternative versions of events. Here too the ego is strengthened in its ceaseless battle with unconscious forces of anger, rage, envy, destructiveness and omnipotence.
- Using estimated percentages for the *weight* attached to different thoughts. Thus to turn

to the girlfriend who failed to return a call, the depressed automatic thought might be 'she doesn't care about me' – weight 90 per cent; the alternative might be 'her phone wasn't working' – weight 10 per cent. As therapy progresses, the percentages assigned to negative automatic thoughts diminish.

• *Reality testing* enlarges on the above, so that the patient is encouraged to confront his negative assumptions and test them out in reality. For example, the patient may equate happiness with reaching the top of his chosen career. He is then asked to consider whether it is in fact the case that highly successful people are never prone to depression or, conversely, whether those less ambitious are always miserable. Again, this is based on the premise that 'there's nothing good or bad but thinking makes it so' and that if thoughts can be altered then one's view of the world will change too.

• The behavioural component of CBT often prescribes '*activity scheduling*' as part of the recovery package. Inertia, anxiety and a feeling of emptiness are often part of the depressive's experience of their day. Activity scheduling involves writing a chart in which the day is broken up into time segments – say 2 hours long – and the sufferer is encouraged to decide in advance how each part should be spent. This may include simple tasks such as taking the dog for a walk, reading the newspaper, washing up, getting to one's psychotherapy session on time or even doing nothing. This counteracts the depressive tendency to see oneself as 'useless' or to constantly measure one's meagre achievements against impossible goals.

- In cases of severe depression, Teasdale argues that CBT alone is ineffective. He advocates combining CBT with 'attentional control' techniques derived from meditation, which, it is claimed, helps sufferers in a more direct way to achieve the detachment from their feelings, which is the fundamental aim of CBT. Here too there are links with psychoanalysis, since Freud's moral stance was ultimately a stoical one, in which he argued:

No doubt fate would find it easier than I do to relieve you of your illness. But you will be able to convince yourself that much will be gained in transforming your hysterical misery into common unhappiness. With a mental life that has been restored to health you will be better armed against that unhappiness[34]

Couple Therapy for Depression

A recent study comparing anti-depressant medication and couple therapy in depression showed impressive results for couple therapy. There are many ways in which a systemic approach can help in depression. For example, the couple is asked to consider in detail the spousal behaviour stimulated by the patient's illness. Often an over-attentive spouse may further de-skill an already hopeless depressed partner. Another common pattern is the 'see-saw' of depression, in which no sooner does one member of the partnership feel better than the other begins to be miserable, and may do his or her utmost to return to the status quo ante. The couple might then set homework tasks that attempt to reinforce positive activity on the part of the patient and encourage the spouse to hold back in his or her attempt to be 'helpful'.

A psychoanalytic perspective on this approach focuses on the object relations stage of each member of the couple and the dyad itself. Where there is poor differentiation between the couple, then each will find it difficult to distinguish his or her own from the other's feelings, leading to an externalisation of internal depressive difficulties and low self-esteem. Thus the husband may see his wife as the abandoning mother who died when he was a child, or the wife may see her husband as the abusive step-father from her past. Conversely, when there is too much separation, neither can provide a secure base for the other, increasing liability to depression in the face of loss – for instance, in the tragic case of a child who becomes seriously ill or dies. Here the therapeutic aim is to foster a separate-yet-together state or, as John Bayley[35] puts it of his marriage to Iris Murdoch, 'learning to grow apart together'.

How Does Change Come About in the Psychotherapy of Depression?

We have considered three forms of psycho-therapy – psychoanalytic, cognitive and couple

– each of which has its own theory of the cause and cure for depression. How can we be sure that any or all of the ideas espoused by these contrasting therapeutic ideologies are valid? There is certainly good evidence that, in general, psychotherapy can help in depression.[36] However, it is far from clear whether it is the specific techniques associated with a particular form of therapy or the general 'non-specific' factors associated with the psychotherapeutic process itself – the attention, consistency, reliability and sensitivity of the therapist of whatever persuasion – that makes the difference. It is also possible that in many cases it is favourable life events that produce change, although it seems likely that good psychotherapy helps people benefit from positive aspects of normal living as opposed to remaining stuck in self-fulfilling depressive vicious circles.

Implicit in this essay has been the view that as well as being a specific psychotherapeutic approach based on transference and emergent meaning, psychoanalysis offers a theoretical framework that can encompass other modalities of therapy. From a psychoanalytic point of view, the key curative features of psychotherapy for depression involve two interdependent and parallel processes. The first is the finding of a secure base/object, and then the loss of that object in a way that is survivable and so leads to grief not depression. The second centres on the replacement of damaged self-esteem with healthy narcissism, and then the gradual dissolution of that narcissism in a way that allows for the independent existence of the object. I will illustrate both with a final clinical example.

Lisa came into therapy in her late 30s: 'I want to come to terms with the fact that I shall never have children', she stated miserably, as yet another relationship had run into the sand. With an alcoholic mother and an absent father, she had found a role for herself as a carer at an early age and this continued into adult life in her work as a social worker. In therapy she was highly controlling and would typically end the sessions herself a couple of minutes early: 'I know how annoying it is when clients over-run.' Eventually she began to relax, to lie on the couch and to let the therapist decide when to stop sessions. Her therapist helped her to see her many good points. She began to feel less responsible for the things that had gone wrong in her life and to get angry with the men who had let her down – starting with her father. Now it was her therapist's turn: she could feel cross with him at moments (they were frequent) where she felt he failed to understand or was insensitive, and began both to resent and survive his holidays (before she had simply accepted that his and his imagined family's needs would come before hers). Her depression gradually receded; she became more self-confident; she formed a good new relationship and, as the sessions came to an end after four years, she remained in touch with her therapist whom she told joyously about her marriage and the birth of her two children.

Comment: Initially, Lisa could not trust or allow herself to be held by her object: she lacked a secure base and her defence was that of role-reversal, in which she projected her own vulnerability into those whom she looked after. With a therapeutic secure base gradually internalised, she could then cope with loss without suffering concomitant lowering of self-esteem. Separation and partial failure became part of living rather than inevitable harbingers of feelings of exclusion and weakness. She moved from the negative narcissism of blaming herself for everything and thinking of herself as worse than others, to valuing her special qualities. Now she could begin to contemplate her vulnerabilities and to forgive others, including her therapist and parents, for theirs.

Conclusion

I have tried throughout this essay to adopt an integrative stance and to give due weight to differing psychotherapeutic approaches to depression, looking for theoretical links between apparently disparate techniques. The distinctive contribution of psychoanalysis has included the centrality of loss, the impact of loss on the internal world and the notion of psychological development from fusion with the object to mature differentiation and the balance between love and hate, loss and internal stability.

This essay started with a contrast between feeling 'OK' and depression. Mood can be conceptualised as existing along a spectrum from depression through 'OKness' to positive feelings of happiness. OKness is the normal state, while most people experience regular but relatively short-lived periods of both depression and happiness. This rather downbeat view is consistent with Freud's statement quoted earlier about the need to transform 'hysterical misery into common unhappiness'. Thus it is possible to distinguish between normal unhappiness or sadness on the one hand and their pathological variant, depression, on the other, and this has been the main thrust of this essay. Similarly, we can distinguish happiness and joy from their pathological cousin, mania, and there too the aim of therapy would be to help the afflicted individual to get in touch with the sadness that so often lies beneath manic elation.

I end with a famous, possibly apocryphal, anecdote. In the 1960s, the then Prime Minister Harold Macmillan found himself sitting next to the President of France's wife, Mme De Gaulle. Eschewing small talk, he asked her what was important to her in life. She promptly replied, 'A penis.' Somewhat disconcerted, Macmillan muttered that at his age he didn't 'bother much about such things'. She replied immediately, 'But 'arold, what could be more important than 'appiness?' At this moment the penny(s!) dropped. Clearly, in his mind there *was* something more important than both sex and happiness – coming to terms with loss, without falling into depression. So perhaps we can restate Freud's dictum. The aim of analytic therapy for depression is to transform it, not just into the capacity for happiness, but also into ordinary human grief.

Notes

1. Styron, W., *Darkness Visible*, London: Jonathan Cape, 1991, p. 17.

2. Shakespeare, W., *Hamlet*, Act II, Scene II. Arden Edition. London: Methuen, 1981, p. 253.

3. Shakespeare, W., *Hamlet*, Act I, Scene II. Arden Edition. London: Methuen, 1981, p. 188.

4. Keats, J., in Stallworthy, J. (ed.), *New Dragon Book of Verse*, Oxford: Oxford University Press, 1977.

5. Schore, A., 'Foreword', in Bowlby, J., *Attachment*, New York: Basic Books, 2000, 2nd edn, pp. xi–xxv.

6. Abraham, K., *Selected Papers of Karl Abraham*, New York: Basic Books, 1953.

7. Freud, S., *Introductory Lectures in Psychoanalysis, Standard Edition* XV–XVI, London: Hogarth, 1916–17, pp. 9–463 (p. 319).

8. Freud, S., 'Mourning and Melancholia', *Standard Edition* XIV, London: Hogarth, 1917, pp. 239–58 (p. 249).

9. Bateman, A. and Holmes, J., *Introduction to Psychoanalysis: Contemporary Theory and Practice*, London: Routledge, 1995.

10. Klein, M., 'A Contribution to the Psychogenesis of Manic-depressive States', in *Love, Hate and Reparation*, London: Hogarth, 1935, pp. 262–89 (p. 264).

11. Winnicott, D., *The Maturational Process and the Facilitating Environment*, London: Hogarth, 1968.

12. Caper, R., *A Mind of One's Own*, London: Routledge, 1999.

13. *De mortuis nihil nisi bonum (dicamus)*. Usually translated as, 'Of the dead, let only good be said.'

14. Pedder, J., 'Failure to Mourn and Melancholia', *British Journal of Psychiatry*, 1982, vol. 141, pp. 329–37.

15. Brown, G. and Harris, T., *The Social Origins of Depression*, London: Tavistock, 1979.

16. Jacobson, E., *Depression*, New York: International University Press, 1971.

17. Gilbert, P., *Depression: The Evolution of Powerlessness*, New Jersey: Lawrence Erlbaum, 1992.

18. Holmes, J., *John Bowlby and Attachment Theory*, London: Routledge, 1993.

19. Holmes, J., *The Search for the Secure Base: Attachment Theory and Psychotherapy*, London: Taylor & Francis, 2001.

20. Greene, G., *The End of the Affair*, London: Chatto, 1952.

21. Holmes, J. and Bateman, A., *Integration in Psychotherapy: Models and Methods*, Oxford: Oxford University Press, 2002.

22. Beck, A., Rush, A., Shaw, B. and Emery, G., *Cognitive Therapy of Depression*, New York: Wiley, 1979.

23. Shakespeare, W., *Hamlet*, Act III, Scene IV. Arden Edition. London: Methuen, 1981, p. 322.

24. Matte-Blanco, I., *The Unconscious as Infinite Sets*, London: Routledge, 1975.

25. Teasdale, J., Segal, Z. and Williams, M., 'How Does Cognitive Therapy Prevent Depressive Relapse and Why Should Attentional Control (Mindfulness) Training Help?', *Behavioural Research & Therapy*, 1995, vol. 33, pp. 25–39.

26. Seligman, M., *Helplessness: On Depression, Development and Death*, San Francisco: Freeman, 1975.

27. Hale, R., 'Suicide', in Holmes, J. (ed.), *Textbook of Psychotherapy in Psychiatric Practice*, Edinburgh: Churchill Livingstone, 1991.

28. Gabbard, G., *Psychodynamic Psychiatry in Clinical Practice*, Washington: American Psychiatric Press, 1994, 2nd edn, p. 273.

29. Winnicott, D., *The Maturational Process and the Facilitating Environment*, London: Hogarth, 1968.

30. Winnicott, D., *The Maturational Process and the Facilitating Environment*, London: Hogarth, 1968.

31. Pedder, J., 'Failure to Mourn and Melancholia', *British Journal of Psychiatry*, 1982, vol. 141, pp. 329–37.

32. Shapiro, D., 'Finding Out How Psychotherapies Help People Change', *Psychotherapy Research*, 1995, vol. 5, pp. 1–21.

33. Lawrence, D.H., 'Manifesto', in *Poems*, London: Penguin, 1963, p. 163.

34. Freud, S. and Breuer, J., *Studies in Hysteria, Standard Edition* II, 1893–1895, pp. 3–311 (p. 112).

35. Bayley, J., *Iris*, London: Chatto, 1998, p. 198.

36. Roth, A. and Fonagy, P., *What Works for Whom?*, New York: Guildford, 1996.

Acknowledgements

Thanks to Ivan Ward, Ros Holmes and Charles Montgomery, and, as always, my patients, for their invaluable contribution to the preparation of this essay.

In case of difficulty in obtaining any Icon title through
normal channels, books can be purchased through
BOOKPOST.

Tel: +44 (0)1624 836000
Fax: +44 (0)1624 837033
e-mail: bookshop@enterprise.net
www.bookpost.co.uk

Please quote 'Ref: Faber' when placing your order.

If you require further assistance, please contact:
info@iconbooks.co.uk